Mayakovsky's Revolver

Also by Matthew Dickman

All-American Poem

Something About a Black Scarf

Amigos

50 American Plays (with Michael Dickman)

Mayakovsky's Revolver

Matthew Dickman

W. W. NORTON & COMPANY

NEW YORK LONDON

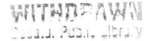

Copyright © 2012 by Matthew Dickman

For information about permission to reproduce selections from this book,
write to Permissions, W. W. Norton & Company, Inc.,
500 Fifth Avenue, New York, NY 10110

For information about special discounts for bulk purchases, please contact
W. W. Norton Special Sales at specialsales@wwnorton.com or 800-233-4830

Manufacturing by Courier Westford
Production manager: Anna Oler

Library of Congress Cataloging-in-Publication Data

Dickman, Matthew.
Mayakovsky's revolver / Matthew Dickman. — 1st ed.
    p. cm.
Poems.
ISBN 978-0-393-08119-0 (hardcover)
I. Title.
PS3604.I2988M39 2012
811'.6—dc23
                        2012018170

W. W. Norton & Company, Inc.
500 Fifth Avenue, New York, N.Y. 10110
www.wwnorton.com

W. W. Norton & Company Ltd.
Castle House, 75/76 Wells Street, London W1T 3QT

1 2 3 4 5 6 7 8 9 0

For my brothers and sisters

Contents

Mayakovsky's Revolver

In Heaven

In Heaven

No dog chained to a spike in a yard of dying
grass like the dogs
I grew up with, starving, overfed, punched in the face
by children, no children, no firecrackers
slipped down the long throats of bottles in the first days of
        summer,
no sky exploding, no blood, no bones
because we were the bones, no more Lord
my God, or maps made of fire, a small blaze burning
right where I grew up, so I could,
if I wanted to, point to the flame that was 82nd Avenue,
no milk in the fridge, no more walking through the street
to the little store
that sold butterfly knives, no more knives, no more honey
now that all the sweetness is gone, though we were the sweetness,
though we needed something
for our tongues, no more cheap soap, no more
washing our mouths out
because Motherfucker and because Fuck Off
came swimming out of us like fish from the Pacific Ocean,
no hummingbirds, no Band-Aids, no scraped knees
with the dirt and rock from the neighborhood
because we were the dirt,
no young mothers smoking cigarettes on the porch
while the sky got pretty

before night came on, though they were prettier
and the sky turned against them. No punk rock, no prom,
no cheap high heels left in the rain
in a parking lot, no empty bottles of wine coolers
because we were the empty bottles, no throwing them against the
    wall
behind the school because we were the glass
that was shattering. No more looking toward the west, no east, no
    north
or south, just us standing here together, asking each other
if we remember anything, what we loved, what loved us, who
    yelled our names first?

One: Dear Space

Akhmatova

That's right! Now I remember. I was on the beach
looking at Haystack Rock,
putting my finger into the mouths of sea anemones,
their tentacles sweeping over my knuckles, I was whispering
the word *brother*
to one, and the word *sister* to the other
though maybe they were both. I wanted to be close
to another species. I had been reading about the dark windows
Akhmatova looked through
to see if her son had been let out of prison. As I walked around
the shallow pools
feeling like I had done a good job being myself
I heard my third-grade teacher
whisper into my ear
what's wrong with you? You want to be stupid your whole life?
She was a nun and wore, I imagined,
a rosary of barbed wire underneath her white blouse.
No matter how long I put my finger into the natural world,
no matter how often I mistake the flies
above the trash for stars, Akhmatova's son will still be chained
against a wall, the sea will still push
against the rock, and a part of me will be sitting near
a window in homeroom, my head lowered, my skeleton warm
inside my body, my brothers and sisters alive in the salty pools of
   the world.

Bridge

Before ever getting to the bridge, at the corner
near the park, two young girls
walk by eating burgers, a mouthful
falls from one of their mouths
and she looks at me, still walking, and says
watchoutyougonnastepinsomefoodyoufuckingfaggit*harharhar*—
I don't know anyone
who would sleep with them, who would
pull their jeans down and lift
their tiny hairs with the tip of his
tongue. Who would want their ass
in his face or the smell of ketchup and pickles slipping into his
mouth. And I can't imagine them
walking over the Hawthorne Bridge, the river
all dark and lit up
like a hero in a vampire novel, can't imagine them
so sad, so torn apart, knowing themselves
enough, that they would
lift their heavy bodies over the rail, one
of their fake jeweled sandals
falling onto the walkway,
and fall into the water below, and breathe in, and turn down, and be
gone. When I stop and look over
I think I'm nervous because I'm worried

I'll lose my glasses, the black
frames slipping off, all the gravity
making them jump, pushing down on them
like a hand on the back
of my neck, what I see: the food falling,
the dumb thumping of the girls
walking, the trees inhaling all night,
the houseboats blinking, all of it happening
on the other side of the lenses. My favorite bridge. My favorite part
of the walk home. This choice
I think I have. In a Christmas movie I like,
a man is standing
on the ledge, looking down into the water, thinking
about it, getting himself ready,
giving people time to talk him back
to earth. Time for an angel in a gray overcoat
and a face from the 1950s to stop him. When I lean over
I can feel the cars racing east behind me, no one
pulls the emergency
brake, no one leans on the horn.
Maybe the girls are passing
in a friend's car, being eaten
up by burgers and flavored lipstick,
the two songs of death

that their bodies are, and maybe
one of them waves, or it looks like she's waving
when she flicks a cigarette, like this, out the window and it falls
    and keeps falling.

Fire

Oh fire—you burn me! Ed is singing
behind the smoke and coals, his wife near him, the rest of us
below the stars
swimming above Washington State,
burning through themselves. He's like an Appalachian Prince
Henry with his banjo
and whiskey. The court surrounding him and the deer
off in the dark hills like the French, terrified
but in love and hungry.
I'm burning all the time. My pockets full of matches
and lighters, the blue smoke
crawling out like a skinny ghost from between my lips.
My lungs on fire, the wings
of them falling from the open sky. The tops of Michelle's long
    hands
covered in dark spots. All the cigarettes she would light
and then smash out, her eyes
the color of hairspray, cloudy and sticky
and gone, but beautiful! She carried her hands around
like two terrible letters of introduction. I never understood
who could have opened them, read them aloud,
and still thrown her onto a bed, still walked into the street she
    was, still
lit what little fuse she had left. Oh fire—
you burn me. My sister and me and Southern Comfort

making us singe and spark, the family
ash all around us, the way she is beautiful in her singular blaze,
my brain lighting up, my tongue
like a monk in wartime, awash in orange silk and flames.
The first time I ever crushed a handful of codeine into its universe
of powdered pink, the last time
I felt the tangy aspirin drip of ecstasy down my throat,
the car losing control, the sound of momentum, this earth is not
    standing
still, oh falling elevator—
you keep me, oh graveyard—
you have been so patient, ticking away, smoldering—
you grenade. Oh fire,
the first time I ever took a drink I was doused with gasoline,
that little ember perking up inside me, flashing, beginning to
    glow and climb.

Weird Science

Because I miss you I have made a pile of clothes
along the bed, your exact height and weight. I've invented
you for a night! I put the dumbbells
of my hands around the sweater that's your waist and let them
fall asleep there. The moon is in the yard
floating through the blinds, becoming a zebra
with glowing stripes, asleep on the floor. In my fourteenth dream
about you we were in Paris. But I'm simpleminded, and also
I want to be with you in Paris! I want baguettes
and petit dejeuners, I want the rue de la Lune and hotel sheets.
French handcuffs and French bottled water. I have
added another T-shirt to you
because maybe by now you've had dinner. In the morning I will
attach a couple wires to the socks and boxers
that are being your head. I'll pull down a big heavy switch
and see if you don't rise up, moaning, your arms out
in front of you, your legs
beginning to kick, and I will hold you up and kiss you
where your mouth hurts because it's new and was only a
    handkerchief.

Dear Space

The woman I love has gone
to bed early
so I can be alone in the living room, alone
in the manic universe of August,
just me arranging
and rearranging the books like someone
packing and repacking their parachute
only I'm not jumping, only maybe the books are not
what's saving me anymore. Maybe now
it's reruns of *The Donna Reed Show*
or the Marx Brothers
or movies about people who are funny
all the time. I keep watching the same rap
video on YouTube
about the stacks of money
and what's going to happen. Outside
it has just begun to cool down
so I can take a walk if I want, see if there's a moon
somewhere above the movie theater,
some summer stars
up there, some planet to go with the grass I'll lie on
next to the school, a big field
where someone is asleep
or passed out, where a dog
overcomes a dead bird,

just half a bird now
but real in the cool dark green, motionless
at the foot of the chain-link
fence. If I were to go out
and find that bird I would want to sit down next to it
and give it a name. I would want to gather up
some sticks and make a house
for it to live in while it's being dead.
I would want to sit there
all night and that's why I'm only going to open
a window, open all my windows, so if it wants to it can
come here and fall asleep in my lap. I'm sitting
in the middle of the room
with a blanket over my head and some letters
I would like to write. Dear love.
Dear motherfucker. Dear heart.
Dear space, I want to write—
Dear space, I can't seem to live the way I should, without
loneliness, without passing out, I keep wishing
I knew more about supernovas,
that I had some of your dark energy,
your dark matter, I wonder
if you're expanding or cooling or what
it will look like
when you turn back toward your own beginning,

what fire, what ice,
what will you invent out there
that Hollywood hasn't already encoded onto a disk,
already built in a garage
off Sunset. But space will never
write back. Neither will love
or real motherfuckers. So I should just stand up, grab my shoes,
walk to the field and sit down
in the grass. I wouldn't be alone. A small breeze
making her wings lift, some starlight through a pine making her
shimmer.

Gas Station

There's no telling what the night will bring
but the moon. That's a no-brainer.
A no-brainer moon sitting there at its desk,
wishing it was outside
on the playground with little Rebecca Steinberg,
her hair around her shoulders
like streamers on New Year's Eve.
The night is going to be a very long night
and I am walking into it
with my sleeves rolled up,
my cap on tight,
all my worthwhileness stuffed into my back pocket
like a wallet full of transcendental credit.
The subterranean elegance of shadows
and the moon like the inside of a jawbreaker
after all the color has been licked off,
all that sweet dye and sugar,
layer by layer
until only the soul of the thing is left, the hard center
that will choke you to death
if you're not careful. Which I wasn't
the summer I turned fourteen.
Anton and I had cornered a younger kid
behind the 7-Eleven who was fat and walking with his little sister.
We screamed at him

Say you're fat! Say it, say you're fat.
And he did, he said it, he cried and said it
and whatever strength he had
as an older brother, as someone
his sister looked up to from behind her big blue eyes,
caught fire between us
and went out like a match.
Later that night I was walking past the Chevron station
on 92nd and Foster,
next to the 92nd Street Club Dancers,
and this guy came out swinging
a gun, his face like an apartment
that no one had lived in for years,
the gun pointing just above my head when it went off,
the moon exploding
and the wind picking up all the pieces
like a mother picking up all the dirty clothes
in a house full of children
who never listen to a word she says.

My Father in Russia

Now he's sending me text messages
from a room full of furs and samovars,
vodka and dumplings, walking
around his living room
in an old uniform remembering his comrades
and The Great War, his medals
heavy, the ribbons float
from his chest to the floor like nightgowns
while his grandmother makes borscht
and his little brother steals copper
wire from the new housing projects.
When he greets me on the street
he calls me Citizen.
Citizen! Hello!
and we duck into a bar
where he changes into American jeans
and a white T-shirt, a pack of Camels
rolled up in his sleeve so you can see
the tattoo that says Lick Me
in Chinese over the head of a cobra,
the red walls covered in mirrors, full
of men with newspapers, some without
their fingers, some
with crutches, an abandoned
television living

the rest of its life in the heart
of the boy washing dishes
in the back, listening
to David Bowie in English. My father
is toasting all his children, the ones he has
never met, the ones who haven't
been born. I keep seeing him
in the eyes of women, in their long
slender feet. I want to walk down
a cobbled street with him, my arm
around his waist like a nurse
heading to the opera. He's getting ready
for the revolution
by not being at all. It's hard
to imagine the body of a man you don't know.
It's up to me now. Citizen!
he hollers. And then I remember. He lives
in Russia, online, I've seen him,
a beautiful bride, a blonde
with lips full of collagen and breasts
that lift up into the heavy gravity of earth,
I've seen him at night
when I've been lonely. He talks
with an accent and will fuck you for real, after
the flight is financed

and a check is sent, oh Dad
moaning through the computer
in a cocktail dress and mink stole, the long
thin fingers, a fake diamond
glinting below a tiny knuckle. I can order him. I can save
the money and meet him
at the airport in Long Beach, I can carry his bags
while he walks behind me
in heels, I can buy him a latte
and English lessons, put my hand on his thigh, fill him
with chardonnay,
tell him I want him and tie him up
with the silk stockings I sent
as a promise of another life,
an afterlife, floating above
the Windsor-green golf courses of Santa Barbara.

The Summer's Over, Jack Spicer!

And Paris, France,
is still Paris, France,
though we've never been there together
but might
if life were a little longer
and no one ever invented knives.
I am crossing the bridge again
and the city is behind me being rescued
or being destroyed
with a leaf on the end of a branch
turning maple-syrup brown.
The first one. The summer's over,
Jack Spicer, and I
have turned my collar up against the wind
and health insurance, the clouds
and blue jays, against the gangbangers
and insufficient funds. It's getting colder.
We're turning from wheat beers to Stouts, becoming
our fathers again, our exhausted
uncles, bruising our knuckles
against the tavern walls
and young mothers, we're showing
up for work, we're blessing
the promise of ice and snow and football to come
like the Israelites did with the sand,

the gold, and the insects.
It's raining, Jack Spicer, and I miss
Matthew Lippman. He's walking
through an alley in Boston,
his beautiful hands and shoulders, his wife and daughter
at home. His heart beating up
his body like a heavyweight, the nose broken,
the ribs broken—
I'm not ready!
Kiss me, take your legs and make a belt
of stars around me,
be my winter coat, my sobriety and bodega.
The oceans are getting blue
and the oysters are getting ready. Soon
we can cover the table with newspapers, with the faces
of senators and crossword puzzles,
the oysters
spread out over the sports page,
we can open the hard shells
and slip the cold
soft bodies into our mouths. We can drink
white wine and make a kind of Pacific
out of lunch. I want to lie around
the room with your jeans
flung over a chair. I want to eat ice cream

and have my older brother back.
The summer's over, Jack,
and all the waitresses
are putting on their black tights like a funeral
of knees, the bartenders
are wiping down the brass, the waiters are drawing out
their lines of cocaine
like long strings of silk, pure white and perfect.
I have crossed the bridge
into a Paris that doesn't exist. Really,
I'm in Portland,
the summer's over and the last of the breweries
are being pulled up into the sky, becoming
lofts, getting roof-top gardens for surgeons and all their beautiful
    brides.

Halcion

You are the illuminated world, floating ballroom, spark and flash,
cold December star above the hospital,
moonlit pond, little boat, your waters calm
as a spoon. I've never been higher.
I can feel you melt on my tongue like a naked girl wearing a
    diamond
crown, standing barefoot on a bed
of ice, her eyes turning white, her body a cloud broken by lightning,
glowing like a nurse in a dark hall. You turn
all my emergencies into cotton, all my fainting into land, my blue-
    eyed boy
at the bottom of a paper cup, you make the meadow
bright, make me brave. Now I can walk
through the land of strangers and freeways, surgery and rubber
    gloves,
the panic, the knife, the ambulance of dawn,
the gurney being lifted into the air. When I'm made to lie down
on the metal bed, when the first tube is threaded through me, I
    want you,
my cherry blossom season, my dream of gauze and light, your
    petals swirling
around my feet, IVs and Jell-O, Tu Fu singing at the edge of the
    Yangtze forever.

Blue Sky

I wonder if it matters that I can't remember
her name, although we kissed on my front porch
in early August and by late August
had taken off our clothes in her backyard.
I wonder if the two of us knew
that I would grow up afraid of needles and the color white
or that she would fall from a window
before taking the exam on 1980s Feminism she had been studying
all semester long, in love with bell hooks
and a boy she met in her Shakespeare class. I wonder if it matters
that she might have jumped, that when I dream
about her I dream she is hanging in a closet. I wonder if it matters,
that she slipped or stood up,
all of a sudden as we like to say, and walked up to the window
and then stepped out,
all of a sudden, but for the hours of sitting
and the seconds of falling,
I wonder if it matters that I loved her when I was fifteen, that her
left breast had three freckles making a triangle
of the nipple, or that she wrote a letter on my back with her finger
so I could never read it
and have only ever guessed what she might have been
saying to me—
this blue sky, our blue sky, this green grass, our green grass,
this trembling ours. I wonder if I'm bad

for forgetting the letters of her name. And then I think
the world is like a crowded staircase
full of midtown commuters all pushing and pulling, each dropping
something important that they will not remember
until it's too late. And then I think I'm an idiot for thinking
the world could be a story I tell myself
to make myself feel better. And then I remember this thing—
I am standing on the top of a building, a friend is opening a beer
    for me,
he says my name, and all of a sudden I'm wondering
if it matters that I am stepping up onto the flat head of a concrete
    gargoyle,
looking down at the parking lot stories below,
and now my friend is yelling my name, rapidly, with a question
    mark
after each time he says it, and I remember—blue sky, blue sky,
    green grass.

Notes Passed to My Brother
on the Occasion of His Funeral

1. My Brother's Grave

Like a city I've always hated, driving through but never stopping,
my foot on the gas, running all the lights,
wishing I were home. Hating even the children who live there
as if they had a choice. I imagine him
in his ten-million particles
of ash, tied up into a beautiful white bundle of lace, a silver bow
looped where his neck should be,
thrown into a washing machine, set on a delicate cycle
to spin forever under the dirt. The all of him
left, the vegetation of him, the no more thing
of him: his skateboard and mountain bike and beers and cigarettes
    and daughter
and mixtapes and loneliness, his legs and feet and arms and brain
    and kneecaps.
Outside the graveyard
there is still some part of him
buried in the mysticism of his DNA, smeared across a doorknob
or brushed along the jagged edge of his car keys. Two kids
from the high school nearby
will fuck each other on top of him
and I won't know how to stop them. Someone
will throw an empty bottle of vodka over their shoulder
and he will have to catch it.

2. Coffee

The only precious thing I own, this little espresso
cup. And in it a dark roast all the way
from Honduras, Guatemala, Ethiopia
where coffee was born in the ninth century
getting goatherds high, spinning like dervishes,
the white blooms cresting out
of the evergreen plant, Ethiopia
where I almost lived for a moment but
then the rebels surrounded the capital
so I stayed home and drank
coffee and listened to the radio
and heard how they were getting along. I would walk
down Everett Street, near the hospital
where my brother was bound
to his white bed like a human mast, where he was
getting his mind right and learning
not to hurt himself. I would walk by and be afraid and smell
the beans being roasted inside the garage
of an old warehouse. It smelled like burnt
toast! It was everywhere in the trees. I couldn't
bear to see him. Sometimes
he would call. He wanted us
to sit across from each other, coffee between us,
sober. Coffee can taste like grapefruit
or caramel, like tobacco, strawberry,

cinnamon, the oils being pushed
out of the grounds and floating to the top of a French press,
the expensive kind I get in the mail,
the mailman waking me up
from a night when all I had was tea
and watched a movie about the Queen of England
when Spain was hot
for all her castles and all their ships, carved out
of fine Spanish trees, went up in flames
while back home Spaniards were growing potatoes
and coffee was making its careful way
along a giant whip
from Africa to Europe
where cafés would become famous
and people would eventually sit
with their cappuccinos, the barista
talking about the new war, a cup of sugar
on the table, a curled piece of lemon rind. A beret
on someone's head, a scarf
around their neck, a bomb in a suitcase
left beneath a small table. Right now
I'm sitting near a hospital where psychotropics are being
carried down the hall in a pink cup,
where someone is lying there and he doesn't know who
he is. I'm listening

to the couple next to me
talk about their cars. I have no idea
how I got here. The world stops at the window
while I take my little spoon and slowly swirl the cream around the
    lip
of the cup. Once, I had a brother
who used to sit and drink his coffee black, smoke
his cigarettes and be quiet for a moment
before his brain turned its armadas against him, wanting to burn
    down
his cities and villages, before grief
became his capital with its one loyal flag and his face,
perhaps only his beautiful left eye,
shimmering on the surface of his Americano
like a dark star.

3. Mayakovsky's Revolver

I keep thinking about the way
blackberries will make the mouth
of an eight-year-old look like he's a ghost
that's been shot in the face. In the dark I can see
my older brother walking through the tall brush
of his brain. I can see him standing
in the lobby of the hotel,
alone, crying along with the ice machine.
Instead of the moon
I've been falling for the lunar light pouring out of a plastic shell
I've plugged into the bathroom wall. Online
someone is claiming to own Mayakovsky's revolver
which they will sell for only fifty thousand dollars. Why didn't I
think of that? Remove the socks from my dead brother's feet
and trade them in for a small bit
of change, a ticket to a movie, something
with a receipt, proof I was busy living,
that I didn't stay in all night weeping,
that I didn't stay up
drawing a gun over and over
with a black marker, that I didn't cut
out the best one, or stand
in front of the mirror, pulling the paper trigger until it tore away.

4. More Than One Life

My older brother is standing outside the movie theater like a man
I have never met. Standing in the snow, looking up
at posters for films
that haven't played in over fifty years. In this dream
he's thirteen years old
and then he's thirty, and then he's nothing. John Wayne
is looking down at him and so is Greta Garbo. Here in New York
Marlene Dietrich is inhaling all the death
a close-up can gather in its big, beautiful, hazy arms. My brother
has lit a cigarette.
He's turning up his collar.
He looks like Gary Cooper. He flicks the butt into the street
like a detective, his long fingers making a shadow
across the sidewalk. In this life
nothing inside him wants to pull a knife, load a gun, open a
    package
of pain killers. In this life he has a day off
and is going to see a movie and buy some popcorn and sit in a
    darkness
he can rise from, and walk up the aisle like a groom, walk
out into the air again, and down the street, and whistle maybe,
    and go home.

5. I Feel Like the Galaxy

You have not died yet. Instead,
you are walking down Thirteenth Avenue
drinking your coffee,
thinking about death, all the different ways,
all the opportunities glimmering
ahead of you, thinking about the woman
who poured your coffee. The woman
at the café who asked if you needed
a receipt, rang you up
and took your credit card,
is a love you will never have
though somewhere in your brain
her long hair is living out
a dream of wheat, her dress,
how it must feel
around her, snug and slippery, is falling
behind you, almost forgotten,
so now you can get back to it, death,
your little love, your hot nipple-action
of fear, a train
in the dark before it breaks, rising up as you
cross the food carts on Alder
and head for the park. There's a garbage can
near the west entrance where you throw away
your empty cup. Maybe,

because you are wearing your new shoes,
you are not heading east
toward a ceiling fan and pills,
toward a six-pack and medicated patches.
I lost you to a bar
and an all-night record store. Lost you
to an old Beastie Boys T-shirt and shredding
punk rock guitar. I found you in a tin can
of cigarette butts
beside the door to the AA meeting
where our sister is standing up and walking
to the back of the room
for more coffee. I found you in my kitchen,
in the handle of a knife, I found you
sitting on my bed, right in the middle, a shadow
made of air and dust. The galaxy's
lifting me across the street. You
should come back from this deep-sea dive, rise
up in your turn-of-the-century scuba gear
while I stand on the prow
of the ship, making sure the oxygen is flowing
down the black rubber tube into the black
of where you are. You should come back
from the fields with your pockets
full of grain, your feet covered in hardened clay, back

from the planet
you discovered but never had time
to name, you should land
in my backyard at night, an earth landing, a triumph
of science and engineering, the rockets
cooling as the door of your spaceship
makes a great sucking sound
and begins to lower, the lights
from inside the vessel
lighting up the back porch and fence and you
walking out in your silver uniform
or in the green and gray body, the silky wet skin
of an alien. I will take you back
anyway you want, I will look into your diamond-
shaped face, into your glowing
egg-large eyes and still recognize you, still
open a beer and sit close
in the yard while you pick at the grass,
staring up at the sky, and cry and scream for missing it.

6. Satellite

I'm sitting beneath the bent
live oak, wishing the plane blinking above me
was a satellite that would shoot images
of my older brother back down into my brain
so I could print them out
and paste them on the wall. I have to
keep looking at this one picture of him
to remember how his jaw was and which side of the moon
he parted his hair. He's always
away from me now, some animal or constellation
that walked out of the world but for rumors
and half skeletons found in the Congo, drawings
of what they might have looked like. My brain dreams
about cities from outer space, a place with a name
like Kilimanjaro where he might still be walking around in his
    Vision
Street Wear high tops, or even a shadow like my father
who talked about Costco the night of my brother's cremation and
    how
pumpkiny the pumpkin pie was
though he bought it in a frozen pack of twenty. Just like a real
    bakery,
he said, you just throw it in the oven,
he kept saying that, you just throw it in the oven, you just throw it
    in the oven.

7. West Hills

My older brother is in heaven
above the West Hills, swimming
in a swimming pool, behind a big house
built on the side of a hill
on stilts so it won't go crashing down
into the long boulevard below it. Built that way
so the house won't jump, won't one day decide
it's over, nothing left, the dark from the evergreen trees
making it all seem like closets and midnight.
My brother on his back looking up at the sky. He's full
of cocaine and Heineken. There is no telling him apart
from the sun or the sky or the shinning stars his hands make,
the water falling from his fingers
back into the wet body of the pool. Whenever I drive up here,
through the black curves, I wonder which house it is,
which one became a kind of vacation
for his heart, what the bathroom looks like, whose bottle
of Vicodin he carried between the soft skin of his waist and the
    elastic
band of his swim trunks, if that person was a woman, if she was
    beautiful,
if later she pulled him, soaking, past the leather furniture,
past the mirrors and Chinese vases throwing up their long silvery
    petals,
into the bedroom and then knelt down

in front of his body which by then was all electricity and chemical
    halos, if
she took his shorts by the waist or by the pockets, if she knew he
    was already
stuffing his wrists with razors
like strange envelopes or building the pyramids
of pills that would take him to Tutankhamun, that he was
    planning his
New Kingdom, if she listened to his breathing all night or if she
    knew his name.

8. Pants

Walking through the snow
all the cars look like flying saucers. Planets are becoming
stars again. The lovers on Mars are spooning
in their beds, their soft green
heads on something like a pillow of cosmic dust. Things
feel dangerous without you and far away.
Space dust floating above
the event horizon, bodies falling from the windows
on earth. Last night
I stopped smoking so now everything will get really-really sad
until my body is done
punishing itself for punishing itself. I have a pair of pants
I work in and a pair I've never worn. I have a pair
I bought in Austin
when the only thing on my mind was Susan. Susan!
She wore these lovely cotton slacks like Katharine Hepburn
but was Jewish
which made her even more beautiful—
some fascist inside me
watching the History Channel and romanticizing tragedy.
Like when they took my brother's body
away and I stood in the house folding a pair of his pants.
I felt so alien and special
placing one leg over the other
and then folding them at the knee like a priest

removing his vestments and kissing the long silk scarf
before gently placing it on an altar
built for a man no one ever knew, not even his father, who wasn't
   there.

9. The Bomb

On December twenty-second I walked out
into the street and said your name three times,
slowly, with my eyes closed, then looked down where the road
stops at the pasture and waited for you
to climb over the barbed wire fence in your bare feet, in the jeans
you wore when you stopped breathing. For a month now
when people say your name I think of a ladder coming up
out of the sea with a small boy
appearing, one foot at a time, looking toward
the coast and then back toward the horizon
and then climbing beneath the surf,
his soft hair floating on the surface before he disappears entirely.
I've been watching a Spanish movie
about ghosts. In it a bomb has landed in the courtyard
of a boys school
but has never gone off, half in the ground and half in the air.
Sometimes
the bravest boys will come up to it
and slap it with their hands. The bomb echoes
and the world gets tested. Men
ride out of a green forest on brown horses
and the bomb just sits there
like an old bell, like a body someone has found
and wondering if it's alive
picks up a stick and pokes it in the leg, the stomach,

the shoulder, the face, and if he's mean or just alone he might try
    to open
one of the eyes, or kick the body to see how it feels, to see if a
    sound comes out.

10. King

I'm always the king of something. Ruined or celebrated,
newly crowned, or just beheaded. King of the shady grass
and king of the dirty sheets. I sit in the middle
of the room in December
with the windows open, five pills and a razor. My lifelong
secret. My killing power and my staying
power. When the erection fails, when the car almost hits
the divider, I'm king. I wave my hand over
the ants bubbling out of the sidewalk and make them all knights,
I sit at the dinner table and look into the deep
dark eyes of my television, my people. I tell them the kingdom
will be remembered in dreams of static. I tell them
what was lost will be found. So I put on my black-white
checkered Vans, the exact pair of shoes
my older brother wore when he was still a citizen in the world
and I go out, I go out into the street
with my map of the dead and look for him,
for the X he is,
so I can put the scepter back in his hands, take the red
cloak from my shoulders and put it around his, lift the crown
from my head and fit it just above his eyebrows,
so I can get down on one knee, on both
knees, and lower my face and whisper my lord, my master, my king.

11. Field

I'm standing in the field
trying to figure out if there was a difference
for my older brother, the first time he cut himself,
between his body as the beginning
of a long, drawn out, war and his body as the end—
a street full of ticker tape and dancing. The moon
is wearing a white kimono that covers most of her
legs. I always knew she was Japanese! I will have to stand here
a long time if I want to learn something, if I want to
transform myself into some kind of superhero for the living,
someone that wears a cape
and fights crime, cures cancer, makes
you feel like you've been bathing in blowjobs and mescaline.
I want, I want, I need! I want the ground
my brother is buried in
to be the field that I am standing on. So we can be together.
So I can bend down
and put my face into the grass. So that
when the wind picks up like Halloween
he'll hear me saying to him *did you feel that? Wasn't that spooky?*

12. Dog

I'm hiding from the stars tonight. I've pulled
every blind and turned off
all the lights but one, which I've named after you,
which I can see flooding the dark
hallway of my high school when I open the locker
with your name on it, the only one
left, the universe flooding out
onto the floor. In all the pictures
I've seen of my older brother
he is never wearing a tuxedo. But I have one snapshot, bent
at the edges, of my twin and me
on a boat, on prom night, happy, already a little drunk.
I carry this picture whenever I fly
so I can look at it right before the crash, below the screams
and the smell of urine, I can look into his eyes
and know who I am. All night I've been worrying
about money and cancer and the tooth
I have to get pulled out before it poisons me. I can smell
the lemon I cut earlier for the carrots and fish. I don't know
what to do with myself. I've written the word *Choose*
on a piece of paper and taped it to a knife. Then I peeled it off
and taped it to a book about Yesenin. Finally
I took it and stuck it on the screen
of my computer where there is a picture of Erika wearing the silver

necklace I bought her. Outside a dog is sitting in the yard
looking up at the porch. Every once in a while
it wags its tail and whines, then it's quiet, and then it begins to
   growl.

13. Anything You Want

My living brother
is treating us to dinner. He opens the menu wide like a set of wings
across the table. Anything you want
he says. His voice warm
above the shinning heaven of the silverware. The other one,
my dead brother, is sitting
in the dark in the graveyard, his back leaning back against his name.
I'm walking by with my favorite drug
inside me. He's picking at a scab on his wrist.
He looks up, opens his arms
wide above the grass. Anything you want, he says. His body
    beginning
to wash out, his voice slowly crawling back.

Two: Elegy to a Goldfish

Ghost Story

I remember telling the joke
about child molestation and seeing
the face of the man
I didn't know
turn from something with light
inside it, into something like
a ship that's just now being
pulled underwater, something like that,
some wave inside him breaking
all over the table and the beers.
It's amazing, finding out
my thoughtlessness has no bounds,
is no match for any barbarian,
that it runs wild and hard
like the Mississippi. No. The Rio Grande.
No. The Columbia. A great river
of thorns, and when this person
stood up and muttered
something about a cigarette, I could
feel the hazmat team
in my chest trying to clean up
my heart, which began to glow
a toxic yellow,
and all I could think about
was the punch line "sexy kids,"

that was it, "sexy kids," and all the children
I've cared for, wiping
their noses, rocking them to sleep,
all the nieces and nephews I love,
and how no one ever
opened me up like a can of soup
in the second grade, the man
now standing on the sidewalk, smoke
smothering his body like a ghost,
unable to hold his wrists down
or make a sound like a large knee
forcing itself in between
two small knees,
but terrifying and horrible all the same.

Cloud

I found a white piece of paper
with your name on it,
your old phone number written in the dark
loop of your handwriting.
I was standing outside a restaurant
watching this one cloud
float by like foam on a pint of beer
and thinking about how good
you've become at not being here anymore, how you
finally broke
like a storm across the sky of everything. The clouds are not moving
in slow motion. In fact the clouds are very fast
and have somewhere to go,
some tornado or other to take care of, to urge on.
This cloud is a rain cloud with a razor
in its pocket. It has followed me around all day
and all day clouds rose above my head and disappeared,
as I lit and relit a cigarette. The smoke
looked like the blue eyes of a fish. A metal
blue ruining the sky, I remember
lying down on the roof of the Portlandia Building,
my high school girlfriend
throwing pennies off the side because she heard somewhere
it could kill a person

if it fell far enough and asking me if I could be anyone, who would
    I be?
I thought of you, lost in a sheet
somewhere, the nurse in her white arch supports,
the trees outside your window making hay
with the sky, your body clouding up, your medication floating off
into a field somewhere full of cows
with eyes and brains and the slow life
I imagine God enjoys
because when it comes to God his hospital is a field, his
    imagination a bovine.

Morning with Pavese

One morning I'll get out of bed
and the piece of glass that has been living in my right foot
since I was seven
will leap from the skin and float along the hall with the dust,
one morning the angel of God will be a woman
masturbating in the shower while I fix her eggs with basil, one
morning only love will crawl out of bed
and everything will be wet and swollen and open windows
with picnics below them and some water rushing by, maybe a white
tablecloth, maybe some silver. One morning
something even better will happen, Pavese will be alive
again. He'll cough up his barbiturates,
wipe his mouth and not be sad. He'll still be a communist
but that's ok. Cesare of onions and Miss. Constance
Dowling. Cesare of cobwebs. Cesare of Nazis. Cesare of the heavy-
     metal 1950s.
He and I will make it rain. We'll walk the streets
and darken the lamps. I'll cry Caesar! with my fist
against my chest, then throw it in the air like a Roman, like the
     German I am.
He and I will watch the sun come up
and make some eggs and make a pact, our razor-sharp love, our
     special victims unit.

Elegy to a Goldfish

I can't remember when
my brother and I decided to kill you, small
fish with no school, bright and happy at the bottom,
slipping through the gate
of your fake castle. I think it was winter. A part of us
aware of the death outside, the leaves
being burned up and the squirrels starving
inside the oaks, the sky
knocking its clouds into the ashtray of the city.
And it might have been me
who picked you up first, who
chased you around the clean bowl of your life
and brought you up into the suffocating
elevator of ours. And I want to say it was my brother
who threw you against the wall
like a drunk husband, the glow-worm inch of you
sliding down the English Garden
of wallpaper, and that it was me who raised my leg
like a dog, me who brought my bare foot
slamming down on your almost nothing ribs,
and felt you smear like a pimple. Now that's something
I get to have forever. That Halloween-candy-
sized rage, that cough drop
of meanness. And your death, only
the beginning, the mushy orange autopsy

reminded us of Mandarins, Navels, Bloods, Persians,
the sweet Valencia. And when our sister,
who must have thought of you all day
came home to find the bowl
empty, looked at us, my brother and me,
I remember we started to laugh. And then
it might have been me,
though it could have been him, who thought to open
the can of tangerines, who pulled
one of the orange bodies out of the syrup, and threw it at her,
this new artificial you, chasing her around the house
screaming Eat him! Eat him!
but it was me who held her down on her bed
and him who forced
her mouth open, and it was me who pushed
the sticky fruit into her throat
like a bloody foot
into a sock. You had only been gone for one hour
and yet the sky outside
turned black and red, the tree in the yard thrashed back
and forth until its spinal cord
broke, and my little sister, your one love, flashed white
and pulsed like neon
in a hospital, her eyes
rolling back into the aquarium of her head

for a moment, and in every country
countless deaths, but none as important
as yours, tiny Christ, machine of hope, martyr of girls and boys.

In Claverack

My friend's daughter is growing up and no one can stop her
but for a speeding car or a lost schoolmate
who finds his father's gun, like on television, inside
a shoebox, beneath the bed.
I hope she lasts forever.
Outside my doorway the fathers
are leaving. They are drinking and singing
old college songs. The ones who didn't go to college
are talking about trucks and the girls they had in them. The ones
     who
became the mothers. A cop is pulling up
to the curb. The sidewalk is leading one child toward joy
and the other toward colossal pain.
Some are playing hopscotch or being outlined by a friend
in yellow chalk. In Claverack
my friend's daughter is thinking about her parents
and thinking about ghosts. In her neighborhood
there are people who have yet to be
born. Their suffering is yet to be invented. But there is time
     enough,
and imagination. There's enough construction paper
and glue for that. The parents
in the doorways have been sad for so long
I don't know if there is anything any of us can do.

Even her. Even if her father reaches down and lifts her up into his sad arms.

But he will try. And she will try. And everything that has happened will happen again.

The Madness of King George

It's time for me to go. I drink
a beer and a whiskey though I should be sipping
Italian sodas, should be home
watching an old movie
or reading a crime novel but I decided to feed my limitations
instead. The woman sitting next to me
calls herself Summer and keeps touching her lips
and scratching her thigh
and ordering a martini
and talking about history. George Washington
and the madness of King George. *He would walk around*
the palace garden wearing nothing
but his crown, crying, holding his gaudy scepter in his hands
like an infant. I am like him, I thought,
and ask for my bill
while this other person, this other
life puts her hand on my knee. *Do you ever think*
about what would have happened if Germany won the war?
she says. Street signs in two languages.
The Jews really gone. And the Mormons, too. Oktoberfest
everywhere. I can see the line
her underwear makes beneath the gray silk. I can see
the wash of freckles on her shoulders.
This is what loneliness is all about. A table
full of bread and wine and you starving but unable to eat or drink.

I think Amelia Earhart is alive and living
in Florida . . . there are pictures of her
walking on the beach. She and Elvis and the Kennedy brothers.
I am peering out from my own grave,
I think, and pay my tab. I put my coat on
and Summer is sliding her long index finger around the rim
of her glass and then licking it. *This economy,*
she says, *the price of gas! . . . It's almost like we're living*
in wartime. I am closing my wallet.
I am stepping away from the bar,
looking at her, stranger now than when we met an hour ago,
when I first noticed her neck, her breasts. But we are, I say,
We are living in wartime. And then her finger stops
and she looks up at me and says *Oh, I know,*
but I mean really, really at war, you know like here, where you and
         I are.

Birds of Paradise

Outside it's ninety-three degrees
so in here it's a hundred and four. If I can be still
for a moment while the woman who loves me is at work
pruning the roses, the hyacinths, the tulips,
while she takes the birds-of-paradise from the dark
box they arrived in and lifts them
into the swimming pool of her arms, lucky birds, lucky flower, if I
    could
just breathe easily like the sound a stone
makes when it's let go an inch above a quiet pond,
then maybe I could pull out
the mean little kid I keep in my pocket for weakness and rage,
    maybe
I could kill him
and in the killing learn something important
about swimming or aerodynamics or the self, the forest of the self,
    and
the city streets of the self. But closing my eyes
here in this little room
all I want to do is be back in my first neighborhood with my head
    shaved
and a friend who can ollie higher than me, who can
skate like Tommy Guerrero
and fuck girls and cut somebody. I want the hazy hot morning
hovering like mosquitoes over the sidewalk

to suck the blood out of my arms—
my teenage mystery and fingers, my skateboard and Circle Jerks
    album,
all those ghosts like birds-of-paradise
being lifted out of the dark
like tar in the middle of West Hollywood—
all those old bones rising up out of the muck, all the new ones
    being thrown in.

Dark

There is a picture in my apartment
where my little sister is smiling over a glass of wine, the dark
glass holding all the red in its perfect bowl
and she is perfect, too, and forever in a black dress
with her brothers spinning out
on either side. I am like you and can't sleep, though you
are maybe doing dishes or watching a movie, I paced back and
    forth
the length of my bed, ate cereal, cried
over the heroics of a cooking show where a southerner
won the weeklong competition
with a pumpkin cupcake. I had forgotten how brave we are, how
    dark
our lives can be, and in the dark how heavy
and full of smoke. I have two coins in my pocket. A quarter from
    Nebraska
and a nickel from nowhere, one for each eye.
One for losing in the street
and one for flipping high into the air of chance. The cold fields of
    Nebraska
and long roads. Heads or tails
on the girl who cuts herself and heads or tails on the boy who's
    beaten
in the bathroom, made to get on his knees

as his fifteen-year-old enemy pretends to make him suck his cock.
    Darkly
serious about love I can't imagine how broken he is,
or how ruined
walking home under the heavy oak trees, or how he'll figure it out—
walking off a roof, stepping up into the closet,
sliding a paring knife over his smooth arm
like sliding a finger along a dark window, the rain and heat from
    outside
making it drip, the water running down, the condensation lit up by
    the moon.

I Made You Dinner, Bob Kaufman!

But you never arrived.
You never called. And that's alright
because I never really invited you. Only you were
gone somewhere in the silent seventies
and I was hungry.
I thought it would be nice
to sit with you and eat oysters or boil some pasta
and toss it in olive oil,
a little vinegar, cherry tomatoes,
some French fromage. I wanted
to look across the table and see you
spreading butter over a roll,
a chicken breast or bowl of cinnamon
and chickpeas
steaming up the space between
us. It was nice, your elbows on the table,
my legs crossed, talking politics
and being sad
because Paul Newman died.
At least I get to sauté
this garlic for you, at least
I get to sear this cod
though you might be
a vegetarian. Bob, I'm ruined.
Come excavate me. Bob,

if we were in Texas
we could eat *migas* and beans. We could run
the hot seeds of a jalapeño
over our tongues and kiss girls
with skin the color of pintos. Let's leave our boots
by the door, let's listen
to the rattlesnakes curl into a circle of dark.
I want everything to do with you
to do with honey
and thistles and edible flowers
like the ones arranged over mixed greens
in California where bistros serve imported water
and lemons from the freeways.
I made you dinner, Bob Kaufman, and set the table
with Dutch china, white and blue, country
scenes and vines. I haven't eaten
anything in two days. I take aspirin and whiskey
at the same time. My body is a boxing ring.
The kitchen is full of puff pastry
stuffed with crème anglaise
and dipped in chocolate, some of them
with a little seed
of sliced strawberry,
like a note that has been hidden
inside the palace walls

some prince might find long after he's king
and the walls have finally crumbled
around him. Bob! You're here
but not here.
The vegetables are all from the market
where the Russians and Poles
are putting potatoes into paper bags, separating
the hard peaches from the sweet,
counting their money,
forgetting their language, missing their popes
and czars, and you
are lifting a single ravioli to your mouth
and I am dipping the wide leaf
of an artichoke into the aioli
I made from scratch
because I don't have to be in hell if I don't want to be.

Canopic Jars

I'm thinking about the ancient Egyptians
and how when someone died
they would separate the body forever in four jars,
four jars all pointing toward
a different place on earth, a different point in space,
and how I'm like a tower
of these containers, how my stomach, intestines, lungs
and liver are all stacked up,
one on top of the other with my heart like a beating
pyramid somewhere in the middle,
the desert of my body
all around it, the great unblinking eye
at the very top
looking out at thousands of slaves, my blood cells,
the long scroll of my brain,
a pharaoh not wanting to die, wanting to live
through each decade, each century
like Freemasons, like *Dollar, Dollar Bills, Y'all.*
My life like the jars too; each love
its own thing, each life
and each death poured into the dark mouth of the limestone,
all my memories, all the nights and the wind
in the night. I want to build four new
jars out of the glycerin rain, out of the atomic
dirt I keep finding beneath my nails

and in each one I want to place a short film, eighteen millimeters
of apology. The myth I have made
of my life is solid gold, a sarcophagus with my face
painted on, it's a kingdom built in the desert of the eighties,
a glimmering nightclub in the distance
where my twin brother is dancing through the hieroglyphic
strobe lights, thinking about a sentence he began
years ago, a city made out of sandstone and clove
cigarettes, frankincense and thighs, French-kissing
and obelisks, a city I'm getting ready to leave, city of organs,
city of rock. I can feel the canopic jars inside me
beginning to tip. When I say I'm leaving the city, it must be
my body I'm talking about, it must be Portland, Thebes, Valley of
        the Kings.

Getting It Right

Your ankles make me want to party,
want to sit and beg and roll over
under a pair of riding boots with your ankles
hidden inside, sweating beneath the black-tooled leather,
they make me wish it was my birthday
so I could blow out their candles, have them hung
over my shoulders like two bags
full of money. Your ankles are two monster-truck engines
but smaller and lighter and sexier
than a saucer with warm milk licking the outside edge.
They make me want to sing, make me
want to take them home and feed them pasta,
I want to punish them for being bad
and then hold them all night and say I'm sorry, sugar, darling,
it will never happen again, not
in a million years. Your thighs make me quiet. Make me want to be
hurled into the air like a cannonball
and pulled down again like someone being pulled into a van.
Your thighs are two boats burned out
of redwood trees. I want to go sailing. Your thighs, the long breath
    of them
under the blue denim of your high-end jeans,
could starve me to death, could make me cry and cry.
Your ass is a shopping mall at Christmas,
a holy place, a hill I fell in love with once

when I was falling in love with hills.
Your ass is a string quartet,
the northern lights tucked tightly into bed
between a high count of cotton sheets.
Your back is the back of a river full of fish;
I have my tackle and tackle box. You only have to say the word.
Your back, a letter I have been writing for fifteen years, a smooth
      stone,
a moan someone makes when their hair is pulled, your back
like a warm tongue at rest, a tongue with a tab of acid on top, your
      spine
is an alphabet, a ladder of celestial proportions.
When I place my fingers along it there isn't an instrument in the
      world
I'd rather be playing. It's a map of the world, a time line,
I am navigating the north and south of it.
Your armpits are beehives, they make me want
to spin wool, want to pour a glass of whiskey, your armpits
      dripping their honey,
their heat, their inexhaustible love-making dark.
Your arms are the arms of nations, they hail me like a cab.
I am bright yellow for them.
I am always thinking about them.
resting at your side or high in the air when I'm pulling off your
      shirt. Your arms

of blue and ice with the blood running
through them. Close enough to your shoulders
to make them believe in God. Your shoulders
make me want to raise an army and burn down the embassy. They
    sing
to each other underneath your turquoise slope-neck blouse.
They are each a separate bowl of rice
steaming and covered in soy sauce. Your neck
is a skyscraper of erotic adult videos, a swan and a ballet
and a throaty elevator
made of light. Your neck
is a scrim of wet silk that guides the dead into the hours of heaven.
It makes me want to die, your mouth, which is the mouth of
    everything
worth saying. It's abalone and coral reef. Your mouth
which opens like the legs of astronauts
who disconnect their safety lines and ride their stars into the
    billion-and-one
voting districts of the Milky Way.
Darling, you're my president; I want to get this right!

On Earth

On Earth

My little sister walks away
from the crash, the black ice, the crushed passenger
side, the eighteen-wheeler that destroyed
the car, and from a ditch on the side of the highway
a white plastic bag floating up
out of the grass
where the worms are working slow and blind beneath
the ants that march
in their single columns of grace like soldiers
before they're shipped out, before war makes them human
again and scatters them across the fields
and the sands, across stretchers and bodies,
across the universe
of smoke and ash, makes them crouch down
in what's left of a building
while a tank moves up the street toward the river
where it will stop, turn its engine off, the driver looking
through a window smaller than an envelope,
where he will sweat and think
about how beautiful Kentucky is. On earth
my twin brother gets his cancer cut out
of his forehead after a year of picking at it and me
always saying "hey! Don't pick at your cancer!"
but joking because he can never be sick,
not if I want to stay on earth,

and my little sister can never be torn in half, a piece of her
used Subaru separating her torso
from her legs, not if I want to live, not if I want to walk
across the Hawthorne Bridge
with the city ahead of me, the buildings
full of light and elevators, the park full of maples
and benches, the police filling up
the streets like Novocain, numbing
Chinatown, numbing Old Town, the Willamette
running toward the wild
Pacific, the great hydro-adventure North
still pulling at the blood of New Yorkers and New Englanders,
the logging gone and the Indians gone
but for casinos and fireworks and dream catchers,
my little sister has to rise from the dead
steel and broken headlights, my twin brother
has to get himself down from the operating table
if I'm going to be able to watch the rain clouds come in
like a family of hippos
from the warm waters of Africa
and dry off in the dust, they have to be here
if I'm going to write a letter
to Marie or Dorianne, Michael and Elizabeth
have to be in their bodies
for me not to cut them

out of my own. They have to answer
the phone when I call for me not to walk into the closet
forever. Right now I am sitting
on the porch of the house I grew up in. The second place
I was on earth! The porch where Emily sat
in 1994, drinking licorice tea
and reading Rexroth's translations of Li Po,
some Chinese poetry
in the curve of her foot, the Han River
spilling out of her hair, over the steps,
and into the driveway
where the dandelions grew like white blood
cells. I would pick them in Kelly Park
and I would walk along the street with them
on 92nd. All my wishes, all of them floating out
over a neighborhood
where I wanted to be in love
with someone, drinking orange sodas on our backs
with the sky unbuttoning our jeans
and pulling off our shirts. There's nothing
like walking through Northwest Portland
at night, even though it's sick with money
and doesn't look like itself. There's nothing on earth
like the moonlight, lake at night
smell of tall grass and suntan lotion. It's hard to imagine

not knowing the smell of gas stations or pine,
the smell of socks worn too long and the smell
of someone's hands
after they have swam through a rosemary bush.
I want them all
and all the time. I need to walk
into Erika's room, over the piles of clothes on the floor
which I love for their tumbled euphoria. I need to
smell her body on mine
days after we have destroyed the bed or ruined the carpet
she hates unless we are on it. On earth
my older sister can never open another bottle of beer, shoot
another glass of whiskey. She can't have the monster
of her body go slouching through
the countryside of her family, killing the peasants,
burning the fields along the road to another sobriety
and then be hacked to death by her own pitchforks and spades,
not if I want to brush my teeth
without biting off my tongue. Not if I want to drink coffee
and read the paper and breathe. Oh to be on earth.
To walk barefoot on the cold stone
and know that the woman you love is also walking barefoot
on the cold tile in the kitchen
where you kissed her yesterday, to be standing in a bookstore
and smell the old paper and the glue

in the spines, to look at a map of a strange city
and be able to figure out
where it is you're going. To swim in the ocean,
to swim in a lake and not know
what's beneath you. To have two thousand
friends on Facebook you don't know
but stare at every night because you're lonely.
To walk through
Laurelhurst and see a blue heron
killing a bright orange fish, lifting it into the suffocating air
and then drowning it again, and then the air,
and back and forth until it feels
the fish is hers completely. To feel how the subway is racing
beneath an avenue
or how the plane that took off from New York is doing
well in the sky over Arizona. To know
how it feels after drinking whiskey or that secretly reading
romance novels has made you
into a kinder, gentler, person, walking through
the grocery store in the middle of the night,
in love with avocados and carrots,
standing in front of the frozen fruit
with the glass door open
so the cold frozen food air can cool your body down
before you walk through the cereal aisle

with it's innumerable colors and kinds, how a box of cereal
feels in your hands
like an award you've received for some great service, to wait
in line at the checkout and not care that you
have to wait. The feeling of being on a boat
and the feeling of putting on new shoes
with a metal shoehorn. How you feel like you can run
faster than you ever have. To get on a bus in winter
and have your glasses steam up, the bus
taking you down the street you have known all your life
or only just found but love all the same. On earth
my mother is talking to her breasts
because they want to kill her, they have turned against her
like a senate, but in the end
she talks them out of it. She makes them behave like two dogs
or like children playing
too rough with the cat and the cat screaming, her tail almost
pulled off. She has to still be here, taking
the Lloyd Center exit to work
in the rain, if I'm going to live at all. On earth
I have a bed I can't wait to get into, the clean smell of white
sheets, letting my head fall
onto the soft pillow and worry and pull
the blanket over, like a grave,
and in the morning watch the cold winter light

blowing in through the window. Every night the dark
and every morning the light
and you don't think Jesus walked out
of his cave, crawled out of his Subaru
and stood on the side of the road for the ambulance to come
and cover him in a white shroud? On earth
I faint in the lobby of the multiplex, pee my pants, go into a seizure
like someone talking in tongues, wrapped
in the flames of belief, my body held in the hands of strangers
above the old shag carpet
while on earth the popcorn is popping wildly
and the licorice is bright red
beneath the glass counter, next to the M&Ms
where the most beautiful girl in the world is standing
in her stiff uniform, her nametag
pinned tight, her name written on a piece of tape
that covers someone else's name.
She will never kiss me, never lie in bed with August outside
and whisper my name. On earth
Joe has a heart attack, his pack of unfiltered cigarettes
resting like a hand near his books.
He rides his heart through the three acres of bypass
and then leads it to water. On earth
I steal flowers from the park, roses and star lilies,
I sleep too much. I'm always too slow

or arriving too early, before anything has opened. I keep
dreaming my older brother
has come back like a man returned from a long, exhausting,
run. I can't do this much longer!
And because I don't have to, I cut an orange
the way athletes do, into perfect
half moons. I peel the pulp away, the skin that looks like
the surface of the moon. I put each one
inside my mouth
and let the sex of it burst into my throat, my lungs
like two black halves of a butterfly
trapped in the net of my chest, I read a poem
Zach wrote about a pond, I'm thinking
about the last time I saw Mike
before he moved into the Zion-air of Utah, I reread
a note Carl wrote that only says
beware. On earth Charlie is cut open
and put back together.
He goes on loving his friends and looking into the mirror,
and maybe the nerves have not grown back
over the river the scar has made, and maybe he is tired
but on earth! He has to get up in the morning
if I'm going to lie on my bed
listening to records with the window open
and the door open and wait

in my boxers for love to enter in her dirty feet
and sweaty hands, if I'm going to pull her near me, my mouth
over a knuckle, my hand beneath her knee, he has to
still be here. On earth
survival is built out of luck and treatment centers
or slow like a planet being born, before
there was anyone to survive,
the gases of the big bang just settling, or it's built
like a skyscraper, by hand, some workmen
falling, and some safe on the scaffold, up above the earth,
unwrapping the sandwiches they have been waiting all day to eat.

Acknowledgments

Grateful acknowledgment is made to the editors of the following publications in which some of these poems have appeared in earlier drafts:

American Poetry Review, *BOMB Magazine* (Bomblog), *The Believer*, *Dossier Journal*, *London Review of Books*, *The Lumberyard*, *The Medical Journal of Australia*, *9th Letter*, *The New Yorker*, *The Normal School*, *Ploughshares*, *Willow Springs*, and *ZYZZYVA*.

"Coffee" appears in *Best American Poetry 2011*.
"Coffee," "West Hills," and "Cloud" appear in the fine press folio "The All of Him" by Lone Goose Press, 2012.
"King" appears in a fine press folio from *Poor Claudia*, 2012.

I am also grateful for the sustaining support of The Lannan Foundation, the Literary Arts of Oregon, the American Academy of Arts and Sciences, and Claremont College.

I am honored to have had the support of incredible friends including Carl Adamshick, Ernie Casciato, David and Joan Grubin, Marie Howe, Dorianne Laux, Matthew Lippman, Michael McGriff, Joseph Millar, Jay Nebel, Lucia Perillo, Erika Recordon, Charles Seluzicki, Diane Wakoski, Michael Wiegers, C. K. Williams, and The Greater Trumps.

Thanks to Jill Bialosky for her trust, insight, and care.

Thanks to my family: Francis Cobb, Elizabeth Dickman, Michael Dickman, Wendy Dickman, Dana Huddleston, and in honor of Darin Hull, for their galaxy-sized hearts.

Notes

"Elegy to a Goldfish" is for my sister Elizabeth Dickman.

"Ghost Story" is for Matthew Rohrer and Matthew Zapruder.

"In Claverack" is for Matthew Lippman.

"Gas Station" is for Dorianne Laux.

"Fire" is for Ed Skoog.

"The Summer's Over, Jack Spicer!" is for Joseph Millar.

"I Made You Dinner, Bob Kaufman!" is for Kevin Young.

"Canopic Jars" is for my brother Michael Dickman.

"Notes Passed to My Brother on the Occasion of His Funeral" was written in memory of my brother Darin Hull.

Vladimir Vladimirovich Mayakovsky (Влади́мир Влади́мирович Маяко́вский) was born on July 19, 1893. He was a Russian/Soviet poet and playwright. He shot himself, age thirty-six, on the evening of April 14, 1930.